STRESS

The Things That Hound You

General Editor
LYMAN COLEMAN

Managing Editor
DENISE BELTZNER

Assistant Editors
DOUGLAS LaBUDDE
KEITH MADSEN
STEPHEN SHEELY

Cover Art
CHRISTOPHER WERNER

Cover Design
ERIKA TIEPEL

Layout Production
SHARON PENINGTON
FRONTLINE GROUP

Seven Studies On Life's Tension

Serendipity House / Box 1012 / Littleton, CO 80160
1-800-525-9563 / www.serendipityhouse.com
© 1995 Serendipity House. All Rights Reserved
98 99 / **201F series•CHG** / 4 3 2 1

ACKNOWLEDGMENTS

To Zondervan Bible Publishers
for permission to use
the NIV text,
The Holy Bible, New International Bible Society.
© 1973, 1978, 1984 by International Bible Society.
Used by permission of Zondervan Bible Publishers

Instructions for Group Leader

PURPOSE:

What is this course all about? This course allows you to deal with stress issues in your life in a supportive group relationship.

SEEKERS/ STRUGGLERS:

Who is this course designed for? Two kinds of people: (a) Seekers who do not know where they are with God but are open to finding out, and (b) Strugglers who are committed to Jesus Christ, but want to grow in their faith.

NEW PEOPLE:

Does this mean I can invite my non-church friends? Absolutely. In fact, this would be a good place for people on their way back to God to start.

STUDY:

What are we going to study? Seven causes of stress (see schedule in Table of Contents) and Biblical strategies for dealing with them.

FIRST SESSION:

What do we do at the meetings? In the first session, you get acquainted and decide on the Ground Rules for your group. In sessions two through seven, you have two Options for Bible study.

TWO OPTIONS:

What are the two options? OPTION 1—This study is best for newly-formed groups or groups that are unfamiliar with small group Bible study. This option primarily contains multiple-choice questions, with no "right or wrong" answers.

OPTION 2—This study is best for groups who have had previous small group Bible studies and want to dig deeper into the Scriptures. Option 2 questions are deeper—and the Scripture is a teaching passage.

CHOOSING AN OPTION:

Which option of Bible study do you recommend? The OPTION 1 study is best for newly-formed groups, groups that are unfamiliar with small group Bible study, or groups that are only meeting for an hour. The OPTION 2 study is best for deeper Bible study groups, or groups which meet for more than an hour.

CHOOSING BOTH OPTIONS:	**Can we choose both options?** If your group meets for 90 to 120 minutes, you can choose to do both studies at the same time. Or you can spend two weeks on a unit—OPTION 1 the first week and OPTION 2 the next. Or you can do one of the options in the meeting and the other option for homework.
SMALL GROUP:	**What's different about this course?** It is written for a small group to do together.
GROUP BUILDING:	**What is the purpose behind your approach to Bible study?** To give everyone a chance to share their own "spiritual story," and to bond as a group. This is often referred to as "koinonia."
KOINONIA:	**What is koinonia and why is it a part of these studies?** Koinonia means "fellowship." It is an important part of these sessions, because as a group gets to know one another, they are more willing to share their needs and care for one another.
BIBLE KNOWLEDGE:	**What if I don't know much about the Bible?** No problem. Option 1 is based on a Bible story that stands on its own—to discuss as though you were hearing it for the first time. Both options come with occasional Comments—to keep you up to speed.
COMMENTS:	**What is the purpose of the Comments in the studies?** To help you understand the context of the Bible passage.
LEADERSHIP:	**Who leads the meetings?** Ideally, there should be three people: (a) trained leader, (b) apprentice or co-leader, and (c) host. Having an apprentice-in-training in the group, you have a built-in system for multiplying the group if it gets too large. In fact, this is one of the goals of the group—to give "birth" to a new group in time.

Beginning a Small Group

1. AGENDA: There are three parts to every group meeting.

GATHERING	BIBLE STUDY	CARING TIME
15 min.	30 min.	15–45 min.
Purpose:	Purpose:	Purpose:
To break the ice	To share your spiritual journey	To share prayer requests

2. FEARLESS FOURSOME: If you have more than 7 in your group at any time, call the option play when the time comes for Bible study, and subdivide into groups of 4 for greater participation. (In 4s, everyone will share and you can finish the Bible study in 30 minutes). Then regather the group for the CARING TIME.

GATHERING	BIBLE STUDY	CARING TIME
All Together	Groups of 4	Back Together

3. EMPTY CHAIR: Pull up an empty chair during the CARING TIME at the close and ask God to fill this chair each week. Remember, by breaking into groups of 4 for the Bible study time, you can grow numerically without feeling "too big" as a group.

The Group Leader needs an apprentice-in-training at all times so that the apprentice can start a new "cell" when the group size is 12 or more.

SESSION 1
Orientation

To get acquainted, to share your expectations, and to decide on the ground rules for your group.

AGENDA

 Gathering   **Bible Study**   **Caring Time**

OPEN

GATHERING / 15 Minutes / All Together

Leader: The purpose of the Gathering time is to break the ice. Read the instructions for Step One and go first. Then read the Introduction (Step Two) and the instructions for the Bible Study.

Step One: Quiz Show. You have all been chosen to participate on the latest TV quiz show. This is your chance to reveal some of your most interesting characteristics and to win some big bucks (funny money) by predicting what your friends are likely to do and choose. Like a TV quiz show, someone from the group picks a category from the five choices available and reads the $1 question. The others in the group guess out loud what the answer will be. Then the person explains his/her answer and those that guessed right put $1 in the margin for their score. Then the person reads the $2 question, and the others guess, etc., until the person has read all the questions in that category. Another person chooses a different category, and the process is repeated until everyone has read a category. The person with the most money at the end wins. To get started, have the host or hostess who has invited you to their house go first by reading the Health category. There are more categories on the next page.

HEALTH

For $1: I can best be described as a:
- ❐ health nut
- ❐ junk food junkie

For $2: I am more likely to:
- ❐ jog
- ❐ swim
- ❐ do aerobics

For $3: My favorite part about exercise is:
- ❐ wearing spandex
- ❐ meeting people at the gym
- ❐ improving my stamina
- ❐ scolding people who don't work out

For $4: No matter how healthy it is, I will never eat:
- ❐ bean sprouts
- ❐ granola
- ❐ liver
- ❐ tofu
- ❐ wheat germ

SLEEP HABITS

For $1: I dream:
- ❏ in color
- ❏ in black and white

For $2: I:
- ❏ snore
- ❏ don't snore
- ❏ don't know

For $3: I am more likely to use:
- ❏ a small pillow
- ❏ a large pillow
- ❏ a bunch of pillows
- ❏ no pillow

For $4: In order to get to sleep, I:
- ❏ count sheep
- ❏ read a book
- ❏ play solitaire
- ❏ watch TV
- ❏ do crossword puzzles
- ❏ wait until I'm exhausted

SOCIAL EVENTS

For $1: When I get an invitation marked "RSVP," I:
- ❏ usually call
- ❏ rarely call

For $2: I prefer attending:
- ❏ a black tie gala
- ❏ a casual cookout
- ❏ a cocktail party

For $3: I prefer attending events with:
- ❏ one or two close friends
- ❏ several good friends
- ❏ a bunch of friends and acquaintances
- ❏ hundreds of perfect strangers

For $4: At a social gathering, I would rather:
- ❏ mingle
- ❏ sing along around the piano
- ❏ go on a scavenger hunt
- ❏ eat dinner
- ❏ make new friends
- ❏ talk about the weather

MONEY

For $1: I can best be described as:
- ❏ a spender
- ❏ a saver

For $2: I would rather carry:
- ❏ a big wad of small bills
- ❏ a few large bills
- ❏ no cash at all

For $3: When I have extra change, I:
- ❏ spend it
- ❏ save it for a rainy day
- ❏ look for rare coins
- ❏ lose it

For $4: If I won a million dollars, I:
- ❏ wouldn't tell anyone
- ❏ would move
- ❏ would buy a house
- ❏ would buy more tickets
- ❏ would not change my lifestyle
- ❏ would tell everyone I was a millionaire

BIRTHDAYS

For $1: For my birthday, I would rather get:
- ❏ no presents
- ❏ lots of presents

For $2: I would prefer:
- ❏ a big, planned party
- ❏ a surprise party
- ❏ no party

For $3: My favorite kind of birthday cake is:
- ❏ chocolate cake with chocolate icing
- ❏ angel food cake
- ❏ carrot cake with cream cheese icing
- ❏ cheese cake

For $4: The game I would like to play on my birthday is:
- ❏ pin the tail on the donkey
- ❏ spin the bottle
- ❏ charades
- ❏ Twister
- ❏ croquet
- ❏ Pictionary

Step Two: Welcome. Welcome to this course on stress management. In this course you will have a chance to deal with some of the issues that cause stress in your life. In this session, the purpose is to get acquainted and to decide on the ground rules for your group.

Stress is one of the central facts of modern life. With all the challenges we face in a world like ours, there is probably no way to avoid it. It has been said that the only stress-free people are *dead*, and that may well be the case! What we need to do, then, is not to seek to avoid stress, but to learn how to manage it in a way that keeps us healthy and happy. Many of us are not doing that:

"For all its action and glamour, today's business world has generated corrosive ways to wear down bodies and spirits."
—*Newsweek*

- Based on national samples, it is estimated that stress-related illnesses cost industry and business $50 to $75 billion a year.

- It is estimated that two-thirds of the office visits to family doctors are prompted by stress-related symptoms.

In the group sessions, we will look at some of the common causes of stress, and how we can better manage stress in our lives. We will do that by examining biblical stories and teachings to find out how to handle stress better in the areas of worry, work, failure, conflict and loss. Finally, we will look more closely at the process of overload and burnout and how to beat it. As you move through these studies, you will find help in managing the wear and tear of contemporary living.

THREE PARTS TO A SESSION

Every session has three parts: (1) **Gathering**—to break the ice and introduce the topic, (2) **Bible Study**—to share your own story through a passage of Scripture, and (3) **Caring Time**—to decide what action you need to take in this area of your life and to support one another in this action.

In this course, the Bible Study approach is a little unique with a different focus. Usually, the focus of the Bible Study is the content of the passage In this course, the focus will be on telling your "story," using the passage as a springboard.

BIBLE STUDY / 30 Minutes / Groups of 4

Leader: If you have more than 7 in this session, we recommend groups of 4—4 to sit around the dining table, 4 around the kitchen table, and 4 around a folding table. Ask one person in each foursome to be the Leader and complete the Bible Study in the time allowed. Then regather for the Caring Time, allowing 15–45 minutes.

STUDY

In each foursome ask someone to be the Leader. Read the following Scripture and poem based on this passage. Go around on the first question. Then go around with the next question working through the questionnaire. After 30 minutes the Leader will call time and ask you to regather for the Caring Time.

> *²⁸Do you not know?*
> > *Have you not heard?*
> *The Lord is the everlasting God,*
> > *the Creator of the ends of the earth.*
> *He will not grow tired or weary,*
> > *and his understanding no one*
> > *can fathom.*
> *²⁹He gives strength to the weary*
> > *and increases the power of the weak.*
> *³⁰Even youths grow tired and weary,*
> > *and young men stumble and fall;*
> *³¹but those who hope in the Lord*
> > *will renew their strength.*
> *They will soar on wings like eagles;*
> > *they will run and not grow weary,*
> > *they will walk and not be faint.*
> > > *Isaiah 40:28–31, NIV*

Turkey Feelings

Lord, am I an eagle or a turkey?
I have all the markings of an eagle,
    but I can't fly.
High places that you promised are
    out of reach for me.
I spend my days here in the valley,
    watching the eagles soar
    overhead higher and higher
    And all I do is flap my wings and
    pretend.

Tell me, God, if you made me like an eagle,
    why can't I fly?

9

"Don't be afraid to enjoy the stress of a full life nor too naive to think you can do so without some intelligent thinking and planning. Man should not try to avoid stress any more than he would shun food, love, or exercise."
—Dr. Hans Selye

1. Which of the two poems above do you identify with?
   - ❏ the Scripture
   - ❏ "Turkey Feelings"
   - ❏ a little of both

2. If you could compare your life right now to an eagle, where would you be?
   - ❏ soaring high—carried along by the wind
   - ❏ feeling a little turbulence—but I'm making it
   - ❏ tuckered out—it's been a long flight
   - ❏ wounded—buckshot wounds
   - ❏ other: _____

3. As far as renewing my strength with God's strength, I am:
   - ❏ starting to feel his energy in my life
   - ❏ open to this, but I don't have a clue how this works
   - ❏ so emotionally drained that I don't even want to think about it
   - ❏ other: _____

4. Which of these situations brings on a "stress attack" in you?
   - ❏ a visit from my mother-in-law
   - ❏ seven straight days of rain
   - ❏ six hours in the car with my kids
   - ❏ a letter from the I.R.S.
   - ❏ my spouse asking me to clean the house
   - ❏ my boss wanting to see me
   - ❏ other: _____

5. Growing up, who did you admire for the way they handled stress?
   - ❏ my mother/father
   - ❏ my uncle/aunt
   - ❏ a very special friend
   - ❏ my grandmother/grandfather
   - ❏ my older brother/sister
   - ❏ other: _____

CARING TIME / 15–45 Minutes / All Together

Leader: In this first session, take some time to discuss your expectations and to decide on the ground rules for your group. Then spend the remaining time in caring support for each other through sharing and prayer.

1. What motivated you to come to this group?
   - ❐ curiosity
   - ❐ a friend asked me
   - ❐ I had nothing better to do.
   - ❐ a nagging suspicion that I'd better get my life together

EXPECTATIONS

2. As you begin this group, what are some goals or expectations you have for this course? Choose two or three of the following expectations and add one of your own:
   - ❐ to find out why I feel emotionally drained
   - ❐ to get to know some people who are willing to be open and honest about their struggles with stress
   - ❐ to relax and have fun—and forget stress for awhile
   - ❐ to see what the Bible has to say about stress and the strategies for overcoming it
   - ❐ to deal with some of the issues in my life that cause stress
   - ❐ to see if God is saying anything to me about my life and his will for my life
   - ❐ to deal with some of the relationships in my life that cause stress
   - ❐ other: _____

GROUND RULES

3. If you are going to commit the next six weeks or sessions to this group, what are some things you want understood by the group before you commit? Check two or three, and add any of your own:

   - ❐ ATTENDANCE: To take the group seriously, and give the meetings priority.

   - ❐ QUESTIONS ENCOURAGED: This is a support group for people who are struggling with all sorts of questions, including questions about your spiritual faith. Honest questions are encouraged.

   - ❐ MISSION: This group will be "open" to anyone who is struggling, and also to anyone who is seeking or who is starting over in the Christian life ... and it will be the mission of this group to invite new people to the sessions.

❏ ACCOUNTABILITY: This group will be a support group. Prayer requests will be shared at the end of every session and group members will be encouraged to call each other to ask, "How's it going?"

❏ CONFIDENTIALITY: Anything that is said in the group is kept in confidence.

❏ COVENANT: At the end of this course, the group will evaluate the experience and decide if they wish to continue as a covenant group.

SHARING

Take a few minutes to share prayer requests with other group members Go around and answer this question first:

"How can we help you in prayer this week?"

PRAYER

Take a moment to pray together. If you have not prayed out loud before finish the sentence:

"Hello, God, this is ... (first name). I want to thank you for ..."

ACTION

1. Decide on where you are going to meet.

2. Ask someone to bring refreshments next week.

3. Encourage the group to invite a friend to the group next week—to fill the "empty chair" (see page 5).

SESSION 2
Stress From Worry

PURPOSE To see that worry is not a requirement for life.

AGENDA  Gathering   Bible Study   Caring Time

OPEN

 ## GATHERING / 15 Minutes / All Together

Leader: Read the instructions for Step One and discuss the various roles you fill. Then have someone read Step Two (Introduction) and move on to the Bible Study.

Step One: My Roles. Here is an ice-breaker from Serendipity's *Ice-Breakers and Heart-Warmers.* From the list, check the different roles you fill in your life. When everyone is finished, take turns answering the questions.

I AM A ...

❏ Father	❏ Mother
❏ Brother	❏ Sister
❏ Husband	❏ Wife
❏ Friend	❏ Pet Owner
❏ Employee	❏ Boss
❏ Landlord	❏ Tenant
❏ Political Activist	❏ Social Activist
❏ Taxpayer	❏ Church Member
❏ Club Member	❏ Student
❏ Volunteer	❏ Hobbyist
❏ Homeowner	❏ Automobile Operator
❏ Small Group Member	❏ Worker
❏ Stepparent	❏ Stepchild
❏ In-law	❏ other: _____

Which of these is the most fun?

    ... the most challenging?

    ... the most rewarding?

    ... the most frustrating?

Step Two: Stress From Worry. A few years ago, singer Bobby McFerrin sang a song called "Don't Worry, Be Happy." It was a simple little song and its popularity was a testimony to the need of our modern world for its message. We live in a world that is filled with reasons to worry: Escalating crime that is no longer just an inner city problem, guns in our schools, child abductions, glum predictions for the long-term health of our economy, ecological crises that threaten the planet, and more! If we let ourselves become preoccupied with worry over all these things, we will drain ourselves of all our energy, with nothing left to enjoy the life that God has given us. But there is an alternative. In the midst of such complex problems, perhaps some Bible teachings might point the way to realizing the hope of McFerrin's simple song.

LEADER:
Choose the
OPTION 1 Bible
Study (below)
or the OPTION 2
Bible Study
(page 17).

In this session, you will have a chance to deal with the problem of stress from worry in your life. There are two options for the Bible Study. Option 1—for beginner groups—starts with a familiar passage from the Sermon on the Mount about worry. Option 2—for deeper groups—starts with Paul's prescription for worry in his letter to the Philippians. Both options use a questionnaire approach to sharing that permits you to choose between multiple-choice options—with no right or wrong answers.

Again, the purpose of this Bible Study is to share your own story, and to become a supportive group. Get set for a beautiful time of sharing!

BIBLE STUDY / 30 Minutes / Groups of 4

Leader: Help the group make a decision for Option 1 or Option 2. If there are 7 or more in your group, quickly subdivide into groups of 4 and rearrange your chairs, so that everyone can participate in the Bible Study and discussion. Ask one person in each foursome to be the Leader and complete the Bible Study in the time allowed. Then regather for the Caring Time, allowing 15–45 minutes.

Gospel Study / Worry Warts
Matthew 6:25–34

Read Matthew 6:25–34 and discuss your responses to the following questions with your group. This passage is taken from the Sermon on the Mount, which Jesus shared with his followers.

25"Therefore I tell you, do not worry about your life, what you will eat or drink; or about your body, what you will wear. Is not life more important than food, and the body more important than clothes? 26Look at the birds of the air; they do not sow or reap or store away in barns, and yet your heavenly Father feeds them. Are you not much more valuable than they? 27Who of you by worrying can add a single hour to his life?

28"And why do you worry about clothes? See how the lilies of the field grow. They do not labor or spin. 29Yet I tell you that not even Solomon in all his splendor was dressed like one of these. 30If that is how God clothes the grass of the field, which is here today and tomorrow is thrown into the fire, will he not much more clothe you, O you of little faith? 31So do not worry, saying, 'What shall we eat?' or 'What shall we drink?' or 'What shall we wear?' 32For the pagans run after all these things, and your heavenly Father knows that you need them. 33But seek first his kingdom and his righteousness, and all these things will be given to you as well. 34Therefore do not worry about tomorrow, for tomorrow will worry about itself. Each day has enough trouble of its own."

Matthew 6:25–34, NIV

1. If you had heard this passage for the first time (and did not know that Jesus said it), what would have been your first reaction?
   ❐ sounds like a hippy from the '60s
   ❐ This person is out of touch with the modern world.
   ❐ This guy doesn't have to support a family.
   ❐ I wish it were that easy.

"Worry does not empty tomorrow of its sorrow; it empties today of its strength."
—Corrie ten Boom

2. When Jesus said, "Do not worry about your life," he meant:
   ❐ live one day at a time.
   ❐ don't plan for tomorrow.
   ❐ trusting God is an important part of planning for tomorrow.
   ❐ God will take care of us, no matter what we do.
   ❐ worry is a waste of time and energy.

3. Which of the following issues cause you the most concern?
   ❐ bills and having enough money to pay them
   ❐ my job and how secure it is
   ❐ whether I'll ever marry
   ❐ whether we can stay married
   ❐ my children's safety, or whether they will ever "amount to much of anything"
   ❐ the economy, or whether the stock market will crash again
   ❐ the lack of world peace

4. How do you usually handle worry?
   - ❒ What, me worry?
   - ❒ I talk about it so much that others worry.
   - ❒ I get busy so I don't think about it.
   - ❒ I let go and let God take care of it.
   - ❒ I worry so much it worries me.
   - ❒ I give in to one of my vices to relieve the pressure.
   - ❒ I get professional help.

5. If you could choose to live a simple life (like the Waltons) with few amenities and fewer debts, would you do it?

6. If you could change one thing that causes you to worry, what would it be?

❒ overspending	❒ my job
❒ my priorities in life	❒ other: _____
❒ expectations that I put on myself and others	

7. If Jesus could have five minutes with you today, what would he say?
   - ❒ learn to laugh more at your troubles
   - ❒ learn to live one day at a time
   - ❒ get out of the situation you're in
   - ❒ take time to smell the flowers
   - ❒ lower the expectations you've placed on yourself and others
   - ❒ simplify your lifestyle
   - ❒ focus more on God's kingdom and less on this one

LEADER: When you have completed the Bible Study, move on to the Caring Time (page 19).

8. Check the two areas of your life which concerned you the most 10 years ago, five years ago, and last week. Do you find any continuity of concern from year to year, week to week? What does that tell you?

category	10 years ago	5 years ago	last week
job	❒	❒	❒
sex	❒	❒	❒
money	❒	❒	❒
marriage	❒	❒	❒
parents	❒	❒	❒
politics	❒	❒	❒
health	❒	❒	❒
fulfillment	❒	❒	❒
relationships	❒	❒	❒
children	❒	❒	❒
spiritual life	❒	❒	❒
retirement	❒	❒	❒

Epistle Study / Winning Over Worry
Philippians 4:2–9

Read Philippians 4:2–9 and share your responses to the following questions with your group.

²I plead with Euodia and I plead with Syntyche to agree with each other in the Lord. ³Yes, and I ask you, loyal yokefellow, help these women who have contended at my side in the cause of the gospel, along with Clement and the rest of my fellow workers, whose names are in the book of life.

⁴Rejoice in the Lord always. I will say it again: Rejoice! ⁵Let your gentleness be evident to all. The Lord is near. ⁶Do not be anxious about anything, but in everything, by prayer and petition, with thanksgiving, present your requests to God. ⁷And the peace of God, which transcends all understanding, will guard your hearts and your minds in Christ Jesus.

⁸Finally, brothers, whatever is true, whatever is noble, whatever is right, whatever is pure, whatever is lovely, whatever is admirable—if anything is excellent or praiseworthy—think about such things. ⁹Whatever you have learned or received or heard from me, or seen in me—put it into practice. And the God of peace will be with you.

Philippians 4:2–9, NIV

"There is nothing that wastes the body like worry, and one who has faith in God should be ashamed to worry about anything whatsoever."
—Mohandas Gandhi

1. If this were part of a speech Paul was giving in your hometown and you were asked to report on it for the local paper, what headline would you use to report his message?
   ❐ Paul Chides Locals Over Scandalous Disagreement!
   ❐ Paul Delivers Upbeat Message to the Faithful
   ❐ Prayer Is Key to Inner Peace, Paul Tells Followers
   ❐ "Don't Worry, Be Happy," Paul Tells Listeners

2. In your opinion, what is the most important thing Paul says about worry in this passage?
   ❐ Rejoicing in the positive keeps people from worrying about the negative.
   ❐ Trusting our needs to God in prayer keeps us from worrying about them.
   ❐ True peace comes from Jesus Christ.
   ❐ Obedience to what God teaches us brings peace to our souls.

3. As you think back over your childhood, who in your family (or friends) lived by this passage, especially verse 6? Did this person have as many troubles as you have to deal with today?

4. On a scale of 1 to 5 (1 = no worry and 5 = lots of worry), indica[t]
how much worry each of the following events would cause you:

	no worry	little worry	some worry	much worry	lots [of] worr[y]
Loss of your job	1	2	3	4	5
Spouse's infidelity	1	2	3	4	5
Your serious illness	1	2	3	4	5
Conflict with best friend	1	2	3	4	5
Alienation from God	1	2	3	4	5
Loss of all your savings	1	2	3	4	5
Your child addicted to drugs/alcohol	1	2	3	4	5
Threat of nuclear war	1	2	3	4	5
Breakup with boy/girlfriend	1	2	3	4	5

LEADER: When you have completed the Bible Study, move on to the Caring Time (page 19).

5. Based on this passage, if you wrote out a doctor's prescription f[or]
someone who is emotionally drained, what would it be?

6. If you were to turn around and follow your own prescription, wh[at]
would be the first thing you would have to change?

COMMENT

Paul now pinpoints the specific problem confronting the Philippi[an]
church. Two of its leaders—Euodia and Syntyche—have had a falling ou[t]
And their disunity is threatening the unity of the whole church. (It is ea[sy]
to imagine individuals lining up behind one or the other of these wome[n]
so that factions develop.) Paul first identifies the source of the disuni[ty]
and then urges resolution of the problem. But he does not stop at th[at]
point. He launches into a series of admonitions, which (if followed) w[ill]
enable them to "stand firm in the Lord" (v. 1). He identifies attitudes whic[h]
help people to cope successfully in difficult times. In the process, Pa[ul]
gives us a profound lesson about the mental state which promotes vit[al]
living.

Our basic attitude ought to be one of rejoicing rather than worrying. W[e]
can rejoice, not because we are blind to difficulties (or because God w[ill]
somehow magically take our problems away). We can rejoice becaus[e]
we know that it is possible to offer all of our anxieties to God in praye[r]
The implication is that God will hear and answer our prayers. In oth[er]
words, God is in control—not circumstances. No matter how bleak [it]
might be (and remember, both Paul and the Philippians were in tough s[it]
uations), God is in control and he cares about us.

CARING TIME / 15–45 Minutes / All Together

Leader: The purpose of the Caring Time in this session is to spend time in caring support for each other through Sharing, Prayer and Action.

SHARING

Take some time to share any personal prayer requests by answering the question:

> *"Where do you need to relax and celebrate life this week …*
> *and how are you going to do it?"*

PRAYER

Close with a short time of prayer, focusing on what people shared above. Go around in a circle and give everyone an opportunity to pray. If you want to pray in silence when it is your turn, say the word "Amen" when you have finished your prayer, so that the next person will know when to start.

ACTION

1. Write down these Bible verses on a 3"x 5" card and place it somewhere where you will see it this week:

   Do not be anxious about anything, but in everything, by prayer and petition, with thanksgiving, present your requests to God. And the peace of God, which transcends all understanding, will guard your hearts and your minds in Christ Jesus.

   Philippians 4:6–7

2. Have each member of the group write down on a 3"x 5" card their first name and the one thing they worry about the most. Randomly distribute the cards, and ask everyone to pray for the person on their card throughout the coming week.

SESSION 3
Stress From Work

PURPOSE

To discover that both work and workaholism may directly affect other area of your life.

AGENDA

 Gathering   Bible Study   Caring Tim

OPEN

GATHERING / 15 Minutes / All Together

Leader: Read the instructions for Step One and let the grou assign each other career choices. Then read the Introductio in Step Two and move to the Bible Study.

Step One: Dream Job. What would you do if you could choose any career Look at the list below and choose a career you would rather do. Feel free choose a career that is not listed. After you have chosen your dream job, le other group members take turns guessing what you have selected.

- ❐ POLICE OFFICER: A brave upholder of the law in an exciting figh against criminals.
- ❐ ACTOR / ACTRESS: A glamorous movie star who gets big money t appear on the silver screen.
- ❐ HIGH-POWERED ATTORNEY: An eloquent, intelligent spokespe son of the law who defends the innocent in the courtroom.
- ❐ POLITICIAN: A high-profile public servant who can whip out a cleve deal or an inspiring speech at the drop of a hat.
- ❐ FASHION MODEL: A jet-setting career for those with a beautifu body and an alluring smile.
- ❐ ASTRONAUT: Daring outer space pilot and extra-terrestrial scientis
- ❐ MINISTER: A beloved servant who takes care of a congregation' spiritual needs.
- ❐ RACE CAR DRIVER: A handsome, courageous competitor wh tears around the track at 200 mph.
- ❐ VETERINARIAN: The beloved animal doctor that everyone trus with their pets and livestock.

- ❏ NOVELIST: The fiction writer who can produce best-sellers that everyone talks about.
- ❏ TV EVANGELIST: An expert preacher and fund-raiser who is the pastor of the airwaves.
- ❏ BANKER: The respected lender who can help someone fulfill their greatest dreams.
- ❏ MISSIONARY: The bold preacher who is willing to go around the world to share the Gospel.
- ❏ PSYCHOLOGIST: The trusted counselor who helps people come to peace with themselves.
- ❏ TEACHER: The educator who inspires his/her students to expand their horizons and see the world.
- ❏ PHYSICIAN: The family doctor who is a trusted healer, devoted listener, and close friend.

INTRODUCTION

Step Two: Stress From Work. Because work is such a central part of our lives, it is also a central part of our stress in life. What are some of the sources of work-related stress? Certainly our list would include things like: time deadlines that are difficult to meet, inadequate pay for too much work, people who are difficult to work with, and an excessive amount of responsibility for the well-being of others. But we should also understand that work which is not demanding enough can also be stressful. Researchers in one study found that people in jobs that require their full potential are more likely to be satisfied (and as a result healthier). The issue then becomes one of balance. Too much work overtaxes our energy reserves. Too little work, or work that is not meaningful, is stressful by leaving us frustrated and unsatisfied.

LEADER: Choose the OPTION 1 Bible Study (next page) or the OPTION 2 Study (page 25).

The following Bible studies will look at the relationship between work and stress. In Option 1, we will look at a parable Jesus told about an employer, and we will have a chance to consider issues like fair pay. In Option 2, we will look at stress from overwork, as well as the issue of the meaning of work. We will do so by considering a workaholic named Paul.

Remember, the purpose of the Bible Study is to share your own story. Use this opportunity to deal with some issues in your life.

BIBLE STUDY / 30 Minutes / Groups of 4

Leader: Help the group decide to choose Option 1 or Option 2 for their Bible Study. If there are 7 or more in the group, encourage them to move into groups of 4. Ask one person in each group to be the Leader. The Leader guides the sharing and makes sure that each group member has an opportunity to answer every question.

Gospel Study / Stress in the Workplace
Matthew 20:1–16

STUDY

Read Matthew 20:1–16 and discuss your responses to the followin
questions with your group. This is one of many parables that Jesus tol
about the spiritual kingdom which God was setting up.

20 *"For the kingdom of heaven is like a landowner who went out earl
in the morning to hire men to work in his vineyard. ²He agreed t
pay them a denarius for the day and sent them into his vineyard.*

*³"About the third hour he went out and saw others standing in the mai
ketplace doing nothing. ⁴He told them, 'You also go and work in my vine
yard, and I will pay you whatever is right.' ⁵So they went.*

*"He went out again about the sixth hour and the ninth hour and did th
same thing. ⁶About the eleventh hour he went out and found still other
standing around. He asked them, 'Why have you been standing here all da
long doing nothing?'*

⁷" 'Because no one has hired us,' they answered.

"He said to them, 'You also go and work in my vineyard.'

*⁸"When evening came, the owner of the vineyard said to his foremai
'Call the workers and pay them their wages, beginning with the last one
hired and going on to the first.'*

*⁹"The workers who were hired about the eleventh hour came and eac
received a denarius. ¹⁰So when those came who were hired first, the
expected to receive more. But each one of them also received a denariu:
¹¹When they received it, they began to grumble against the landowne
¹²'These men who were hired last worked only one hour,' they said, 'and yo
have made them equal to us who have borne the burden of the work an
the heat of the day.'*

*¹³"But he answered one of them, 'Friend, I am not being unfair to yo
Didn't you agree to work for a denarius? ¹⁴Take your pay and go. I want i
give the man who was hired last the same as I gave you. ¹⁵Don't I have th
right to do what I want with my own money? Or are you envious because
am generous?'*

¹⁶"So the last will be first, and the first will be last."

Matthew 20:1–16, NI

1. If someone had told you this story during coffee break at wor
   what would have been your first reaction?
   - ❏ This is a fantasy world.
   - ❏ Those last guys must have had a good union.
   - ❏ Where do I sign up to work for that guy?
   - ❏ Typical boss—seniority means nothing.
   - ❏ He's the boss—he can do whatever he wants.

2. If you were one of the first workers hired, how would you have reacted to the landowner?
   ❏ I wouldn't have complained, because I got the pay I agreed to.
   ❏ I would have reported him to the Jerusalem Better Business Bureau.
   ❏ I would never work for him again.
   ❏ I would have complained about him and berated him.
   ❏ I would have picketed his business.

3. What were the unmet expectations of the first workers, which created a conflict with the landowner?
   ❏ They expected more money for more work.
   ❏ They expected to get paid for doing little work.
   ❏ They expected the landowner to be fair.
   ❏ They expected the landowner to do whatever he wanted.

"I may be a lousy father and a lousy husband, but when Merrill ynch needs me, I'm here."
—a stockbroker

4. What was your very first job? How much money did you make?

5. Which employer has been the most generous in their compensation to you? The most stingy?

6. What expectations regarding compensation do you have of your employer?
   ❏ If I go the "extra mile," I expect to be rewarded.
   ❏ No matter what I do, I will get paid the same.
   ❏ I work for rewards other than money.
   ❏ Employers are never fair and never will be.
   ❏ I expect equal pay for equal work.

7. What is the main reason you work?
   ❏ to survive
   ❏ to give our children and grandchildren a better life
   ❏ I'd be bored otherwise.
   ❏ to obtain material goods
   ❏ because work is "meaningful"

8. While work can certainly be satisfying, it can also be stressful. Which of the following do you consider to be the most stressful in the workplace?
   ❏ an excessive workload   ❏ job insecurity
   ❏ an unreasonable boss   ❏ unfriendly coworkers
   ❏ monotonous work   ❏ low pay

9. Few work situations, whether at home or in the workplace, are free of stress. With the help of the following list, indicate the ways you usually manage stress. Of these ways, which one(s) work(s) best for you?

❐ I exercise regularly.
❐ I take naps regularly.
❐ I rant, rave, and cry a lot.
❐ I participate in sports/hobbies.
❐ I get out into nature.
❐ I pray for the ability to handle stress.
❐ I use mind relaxation techniques.
❐ I pour my heart out to God.
❐ I get professional counseling.
❐ I don't manage stress, it manages me.
❐ I take tranquilizers and/or drink alcohol to relax.
❐ I ignore stress.
❐ I take regular vacations.
❐ I watch TV or movies to escape.
❐ I read to escape and relax.
❐ I redouble my efforts and work harder.
❐ I spend some time alone.
❐ I play as often as I can.
❐ I listen to my favorite music.
❐ I read and study the Bible.
❐ I buy myself something new.
❐ I talk to others about stressful situations.
❐ I draw support and strength from others.

LEADER: When you have completed the Bible Study, move on to the Caring Time (page 28).

COMMENT

This is a parable about a "large-hearted man who is compassionate and full of sympathy for the poor" (Jeremias). "The essential point of the parable is that God is like that; his generosity transcends human ideas of fairness. No one receives less than they deserve, but some receive far more" (R.T. France).

We learn from this parable that God's standards are not our standards. Hard work and high reward are not equal in his kingdom. After all, it is all grace. We also note that the work-related stress in this passage is a matter of an understandable (but harmful) *attitude*. The stress does not come because the workers are cheated by the boss; everyone gets a fair wage. The stress comes from jealousy—some get the same wage for less work than others. Sometimes it is our attitude that needs changing in order to relieve stress. Even in an exploitative situation, the answer may be to change our attitude (e.g., to confront the problem regardless of cost, to deal directly and openly instead of backbiting—to find our own satisfaction in the job).

Epistle Study / The Workaholic
2 Corinthians 11:16–33

Read 2 Corinthians 11:16–33 and discuss your responses to the following questions with your group. This is taken from the writings of the apostle Paul, who is defending his life and work.

[16]*I repeat: Let no one take me for a fool. But if you do, then receive me just as you would a fool, so that I may do a little boasting.* [17]*In this self-confident boasting I am not talking as the Lord would, but as a fool.* [18]*Since many are boasting in the way the world does, I too will boast.* [19]*You gladly put up with fools since you are so wise!* [20]*In fact, you even put up with anyone who enslaves you or exploits you or takes advantage of you or pushes himself forward or slaps you in the face.* [21]*To my shame I admit that we were too weak for that!*

What anyone else dares to boast about—I am speaking as a fool—I also dare to boast about. [22]*Are they Hebrews? So am I. Are they Israelites? So am I. Are they Abraham's descendants? So am I.* [23]*Are they servants of Christ? (I am out of my mind to talk like this.) I am more. I have worked much harder, been in prison more frequently, been flogged more severely, and been exposed to death again and again.* [24]*Five times I received from the Jews the forty lashes minus one.* [25]*Three times I was beaten with rods, once I was stoned, three times I was shipwrecked, I spent a night and a day in the open sea,* [26]*I have been constantly on the move. I have been in danger from rivers, in danger from bandits, in danger from my own countrymen, in danger from Gentiles; in danger in the city, in danger in the country, in danger at sea; and in danger from false brothers.* [27]*I have labored and toiled and have often gone without sleep; I have known hunger and thirst and have often gone without food; I have been cold and naked.* [28]*Besides everything else, I face daily the pressure of my concern for all the churches.* [29]*Who is weak, and I do not feel weak? Who is led into sin, and I do not inwardly burn?*

[30]*If I must boast, I will boast of the things that show my weakness.* [31]*The God and Father of the Lord Jesus, who is to be praised forever, knows that I am not lying.* [32]*In Damascus the governor under King Aretas had the city of the Damascenes guarded in order to arrest me.* [33]*But I was lowered in a basket from a window in the wall and slipped through his hands.*

2 Corinthians 11:16–33, NIV

1. Of the four temperaments, which temperament describes Pau best?
   - ❐ SANGUINE: Super salesperson. Warm. Outgoing. Happy-go lucky on the surface. Charmer.
   - ❐ CHOLERIC: Super leader. Assertive. Self-willed drive Crusader. Task-oriented. Entrepreneur.
   - ❐ MELANCHOLIC: Super sensitive. Creative. Imaginative. Love of peace and quiet. Artistic.
   - ❐ PHLEGMATIC: Super laid-back. Likable. Dependable. Practica Conservative. Easygoing.

2. Why do you think Paul drove himself like he did?
   - ❐ His toilet training was too strict.
   - ❐ a desire to prove himself
   - ❐ masochism
   - ❐ love for the people he worked with
   - ❐ a deep sense of his calling to spread the Gospel
   - ❐ other:_____

3. How would you compare your work habits with Paul's?
   - ❐ Our work habits are very similar.
   - ❐ Paul is a lot more driven than I am.
   - ❐ I am a lot more driven than Paul.
   - ❐ It all depends upon the work I'm doing.
   - ❐ other:_____

4. How would Paul fit into your office or work?
   - ❐ He would drive us crazy.
   - ❐ He would be good for us.
   - ❐ He would dominate the dicussion at lunch.
   - ❐ He would fit right in with the rest of us.
   - ❐ He would have to be the boss.
   - ❐ He would make the rest of us look bad.
   - ❐ other: _____

5. How would you like to have Paul as your boss?
   - ❐ I would love it.
   - ❐ It would be a real challenge.
   - ❐ It would be good for me.
   - ❐ I already work for someone like that.
   - ❐ It probably would be good for the company, but hard on me.
   - ❐ other:_____

"My father taught me to work, but not to love it. I never did like to work, and I don't deny it. I'd rather read, tell stories, crack jokes, talk, laugh—anything but work."
—Abraham Lincoln

26

LEADER: When you have completed the Bible Study, move on to the Caring Time (page 28).

6. Which temperament are you at work?
   ❏ sanguine
   ❏ choleric
   ❏ melancholic
   ❏ phlegmatic

7. Why do you work hard? (choose two)
   ❏ to feel good about myself
   ❏ I don't know how to slow down.
   ❏ to please others
   ❏ I was brought up to be this way.
   ❏ to fulfill a calling
   ❏ I am driven by a desire to be successful.
   ❏ to avoid relationships and responsibilities
   ❏ I have a fear of failure.
   ❏ It seems like the right thing to do.
   ❏ God expects it of me.
   ❏ I don't work all that hard.

8. On the following scale, how would you evaluate the amount of time and emotional energy you give to work?

1	2	3	4	5	6	7	8	9	10
far too little				just right					far too much

9. On the following scale, how would you evaluate the amount of meaning you get out of work?

1	2	3	4	5	6	7	8	9	10
far too little				just right					far too much

CARING TIME / 15–45 Minutes / All Together

Leader: Bring all of the foursomes back together for a time c caring support for one another. Be sensitive to what the other share during this Caring Time.

SHARING

Take some time to share any personal prayer requests and answer th question:

*"If you knew you could not fail,
what would you like to change about your work or career?"*

PRAYER

Close with a short time of prayer, remembering the dreams that hav been shared. If you would like to pray in silence, say the word "Amer when you have finished your prayer, so that the next person will kno when to start.

ACTION

Turn to the person next to you and tell them one thing you want to chang this week to reduce the stress level at your work or home situation. Fc example: "I will be extra kind to my spouse or a difficult coworker," or won't work overtime this week and I'll take all my lunch breaks Throughout the coming week, be in prayer for each other.

SESSION 4
Stress From Failure

PURPOSE

To understand that although stress is connected with avoiding failure, failure is often a prerequisite for success.

AGENDA

 Gathering   Bible Study   Caring Time

OPEN

GATHERING / 15 Minutes / All Together

Leader: Read the instructions for Step One. Set the pace by going first on "My Family Table." Before the meeting, draw the shape of your table on a sheet of paper and "show and tell" it—with colors—so that everyone knows what to do. The way you explain the colors you choose for your father and mother will make or break this exercise. Then read Step Two (Introduction) and move on to the Bible Study.

Step One: My Family Table. Try to recall the table where you ate most of your meals as a child, and the people who sat around that table. Use the questions below to describe these significant relationships, and how they helped to shape the person you are today.

1. What was the shape of the table?
2. Where did you sit?
3. Who else was at the table?
4. If you had to describe each person with a color, what would be the color of (for instance):
   ❑ your father? (i.e., dark blue, because he was conservative like IBM)
   ❑ your mother? (i.e., light green, because she reminded me of springtime)
5. If you had to describe the atmosphere at the table with a color, what would you choose? (i.e., bright orange, because it was light and warm)
6. Which person at your childhood table praised you and made you feel special?
7. If you could brag about one thing you excelled at as a child, what would you brag about?

Step Two: Stress From Failure. The message is the same: making it is what life is all about. Not surprisingly, stress is connected with avoiding failure. All of us have failed at one time or another. Failure really isn't much fun. But if we fear failure, we can be immobilized and will avoid anything that involves a degree of risk.

We can learn much through failure. Often failure is a prerequisite to success. The stories of successful people invariably tell us that they have failed one or more times before they became successful. Abraham Lincoln considered himself to be a failure in the eyes of his contemporaries. Thomas Edison failed repeatedly before he lit his first incandescent bulb. Marie Curie persevered despite financial, scientific and health setbacks. Winston Churchill gives us a perspective on failure when he said, "Success is going from failure to failure without loss of enthusiasm."

LEADER:
Choose the
OPTION 1 Bible
Study (below)
or the OPTION 2
Study (page 33).

In Option 1 (from Luke's Gospel), Peter painfully learns some deeper truths through failure. In Option 2 (from Paul's letter to the Romans), the apostle experiences some failure in his inner battle between good and evil. Both studies will help us to rise above failure. Remember, the purpose of the Bible Study is to share your own story. Use this opportunity to deal with issues in your life in this support group.

BIBLE STUDY / 30 Minutes / Groups of 4

Leader: Help the group decide on an Option 1 or Option Bible Study. If there are more than 7 people, divide into groups of 4, and ask one person in each group to be the Leader. Finish the Bible Study in 30 minutes, and gather the groups together for the Caring Time.

OPTION 1

Gospel Study / Fear of Failure
Luke 22:54–62

STUDY

Read Luke 22:54–62 and discuss your responses to the following questions with your group. This story describes the experience of one Jesus' disciples on the night that Jesus was arrested and taken away be crucified.

54Then seizing him [Jesus], they [the temple police] led him away and took him into the house of the high priest. Peter followed at a distance. **55**But when they had kindled a fire in the middle of the courtyard and had sat down together, Peter sat down with them. **56**A servant girl saw him seated there in the firelight. She looked closely at him and said, "This man was with him."

57But he denied it. "Woman, I don't know him," he said.

58A little later someone else saw him and said, "You also are one of them."

"Man, I am not!" Peter replied.

59About an hour later another asserted, "Certainly this fellow was with him, for he is a Galilean."

60Peter replied, "Man, I don't know what you're talking about!" Just as he was speaking, the rooster crowed. **61**The Lord turned and looked straight at Peter. Then Peter remembered the word the Lord had spoken to him: "Before the rooster crows today, you will disown me three times." **62**And he went outside and wept bitterly.

Luke 22:54–62, NIV

"Often we assume that God is unable to work in spite of our weaknesses, mistakes, and sins. We forget that God is a specialist; he is able to work our failures into his plans."
—Erwin W. Lutzer

1. If you could put in a good word for Peter from this event, what would it be?
   ❏ He meant well.   ❏ He's only human.
   ❏ He couldn't help it.   ❏ He was confused.
   ❏ He came back.   ❏ other: _____

2. Why did Peter keep at a distance and deny his association with Jesus?
   ❏ He didn't want to get involved.
   ❏ He didn't want to get into trouble with the authorities.
   ❏ He was confused about who Jesus was.
   ❏ He was trying to devise an escape plan.

3. If you were in Peter's shoes, how would you have reacted?
   ❏ I would have kept my mouth shut.
   ❏ I would have gone home.
   ❏ I would have done the same as Peter.
   ❏ I would have argued Jesus' case.
   ❏ other: _____

4. How do you think Peter felt when Jesus looked at him?
   ❏ He realized how stupid he had been.
   ❏ He felt ashamed of his behavior.
   ❏ He was unaffected by the whole matter.
   ❏ He was humiliated by his failure.

5. If you had been Jesus, would you have removed Peter from the team because of his failure?
   ❏ Yes
   ❏ No—but I would have put him on probation.
   ❏ No—I think it helped shape his future.
   ❏ Maybe—it all depends on Peter's response.

6. How do you generally react when you experience failure?
   ❏ I try to learn from my failures.
   ❏ I try to ignore and forget my failures.
   ❏ I am emotionally wounded by failure.
   ❏ I accept failure as a reality of life.
   ❏ I don't want to try again when I fail.
   ❏ I refuse to accept failure in anything I do.

7. How has failure in your life changed you?
   ❏ I am now more caring and empathetic.
   ❏ I am now more determined than ever.
   ❏ I am now more humble.
   ❏ I now look out for myself more.
   ❏ I am now more realistic.
   ❏ I am now emotionally fragile.
   ❏ I am now confused and disillusioned.
   ❏ I am now wiser.
   ❏ other: _____

LEADER: When you have completed the Bible Study, move on to the Caring Time (page 36).

8. What lesson or principle would you like to pass on to your kids in dealing with failure?

COMMENT

Talk about failure ... It was bad enough that Peter denied Jesus, but worse coming right on the heels of his boast: "Even if I have to die with you, I will never disown you" (Mark 14:31). However, it is probably that experience that opened Peter's eyes to himself and made it possible for him to come to Jesus in repentance and faith. His failure did not affect his relationship with Jesus. The angel at the tomb makes a point of saying, "Go, tell the disciples *and* Peter, 'He is going ahead of you in Galilee. There you will see him' " (Mark 16:7). His failure did not affect Peter's role in the church. He became one of its pillars (Gal. 2:7–9). For the Christian failure is not the end. It is often the beginning of new ministry, because it is in our weakness that we are made strong (Rom. 8:26; 1 Cor. 2:1).

Epistle Study / Fail-Safe
Romans 7:7–25

STUDY

Read Romans 7:7–25 and discuss your responses to the following questions with your group. This in-depth passage talks about the relative roles of the Jewish Law. It also highlights God's forgiveness and grace in bringing people into a healing relationship with himself.

⁷What shall we say, then? Is the law sin? Certainly not! Indeed I would not have known what sin was except through the law. For I would not have known what coveting really was if the law had not said, "Do not covet." ⁸But sin, seizing the opportunity afforded by the commandment, produced in me every kind of covetous desire. For apart from law, sin is dead. ⁹Once I was alive apart from law; but when the commandment came, sin sprang to life and I died. ¹⁰I found that the very commandment that was intended to bring life actually brought death. ¹¹For sin, seizing the opportunity afforded by the commandment, deceived me, and through the commandment put me to death. ¹²So then, the law is holy, and the commandment is holy, righteous and good.

¹³Did that which is good, then, become death to me? By no means! But in order that sin might be recognized as sin, it produced death in me through what was good, so that through the commandment sin might become utterly sinful.

¹⁴We know that the law is spiritual; but I am unspiritual, sold as a slave to sin. ¹⁵I do not understand what I do. For what I want to do I do not do, but what I hate I do. ¹⁶And if I do what I do not want to do, I agree that the law is good. ¹⁷As it is, it is no longer I myself who do it, but it is sin living in me. ¹⁸I know that nothing good lives in me, that is, in my sinful nature. For I have the desire to do what is good, but I cannot carry it out. ¹⁹For what I do is not the good I want to do; no, the evil I do not want to do—this I keep on doing. ²⁰Now if I do what I do not want to do, it is no longer I who do it, but it is sin living in me that does it.

²¹So I find this law at work: When I want to do good, evil is right there with me. ²²For in my inner being I delight in God's law; ²³but I see another law at work in the members of my body, waging war against the law of my mind and making me a prisoner of the law of sin at work within my members. ²⁴What a wretched man I am! Who will rescue me from this body of death? ²⁵Thanks be to God—through Jesus Christ our Lord!

So then, I myself in my mind am a slave to God's law, but in the sinful nature a slave to the law of sin.

Romans 7:7–25, NIV

1. How would you describe the apostle Paul in this passage?
   - ❐ schizophrenic
   - ❐ a little disturbed
   - ❐ a bit distraught
   - ❐ confused
   - ❐ emotionally wiped out
   - ❐ just being honest

"Failure sometimes enlarges the spirit. You have to fall back upon humanity and God."
—Charles H. Cooley

2. What does Paul mean when he says that, "apart from law, sin is dead" (v. 8)?
   - ❐ If you sin and no one catches you, you're not guilty.
   - ❐ If God hadn't give us his commandments, there would be no right and wrong.
   - ❐ You can only determine right and wrong by listening to God's definition of sin.
   - ❐ If people reject God, nothing is sinful in their eyes.

3. What does Paul mean by saying that the Law is spiritual (v. 14)?
   - ❐ The Law is something only angels understand.
   - ❐ The Law is from God and reflects who he is.
   - ❐ The Law can't be separated from God.
   - ❐ The Law hasn't ever changed and never will—because God doesn't change.
   - ❐ People who say that right and wrong can only be decided by the individual are denying that God's definition of right and wrong is the only true one.

4. What truth about sin is Paul declaring when he shares about his own frustrations with sin in verses 14–25?
   - ❐ Sin is powerful—it will try to control us any way it can.
   - ❐ Without God's presence in our life, it's easy for sin to take over without us ever even feeling guilty.
   - ❐ We will never be able to do good on our own—sin will always win out. Only through God can we do what is good.
   - ❐ Even "super Christians" like Paul get frustrated and feel like failures sometimes.

5. How would you compare your self-understanding to Paul's self-understanding in this passage?
   - ❐ He's more open about his struggles than I am.
   - ❐ He's more in touch with his struggles than I am.
   - ❐ He and I are very much alike.
   - ❐ I'm not really sure where I am—I've never stopped to think about it.

LEADER: When you have completed the Bible Study, move on to the Caring Time (page 36).

6. Do you think Paul was a failure because of his struggles?
   - ❐ Yes
   - ❐ Well, he needs help.
   - ❐ Maybe—he sounds depressed.
   - ❐ No—he is on the road to recovery.

7. If you could give Paul a word of advice based on your experience, what would you say?
   - ❐ It's okay to be down on yourself, just so you don't wallow in it.
   - ❐ Recovery began for me when I made a "searching moral inventory" of my life.
   - ❐ We're all human. Thanks to Jesus, we're saved in spite of all our failures.
   - ❐ This is too deep for me.
   - ❐ other: _____

8. How is Paul (and are all of us) rescued from this struggle with sin?
   - ❐ We aren't rescued permanently (until heaven), but the struggle is easier.
   - ❐ We struggle, but with Jesus in our life he is always in control.
   - ❐ We love to sin and it shows.
   - ❐ I don't struggle with sin.
   - ❐ There is no such thing as sin, simply "errors in judgment."

COMMENT

There is an inner principle in all people that inclines them to failure. Failure is normal; success is the surprise. Here Paul identifies the reason for this: it is sin dwelling in us. And the word sin in the New Testament refers not just to active transgression, but also to falling short of what should be (i.e., failure). But Paul does not end with this fact. He goes on in Romans 8 to describe the freedom from sin and death brought about by the Spirit of God.

CARING TIME / 15–45 Minutes / All Together

Leader: Bring all of the foursomes back together for a time of caring through Sharing, Prayer and Action. Remember to be sensitive as people share about their failures.

SHARING

Alcoholics Anonymous recommends a 12-step process for recovery. Step #5 is to make a moral inventory of your failures, and walk through this list with another person "in confession."

If you were to review your life and pinpoint your "failures" that have crippled your life, where would you begin? Is this something you have to deal with? Is this something that this group could help you deal with? If anybody wants to share, give them your heart.

Go around in your group and allow everyone to finish this sentence:

*"The area in my life where I struggled the most
with a sense of failure was ..."*

as a child ...

as an adolescent ...

as an adult ...

PRAYER

During your time of prayer, remember the people who shared and what they said. If you don't know how to begin, finish this sentence:

"Lord, I want to talk with you about my friend ..."

ACTION

1. Write these verses of Scripture on a 3" x 5" card and put it on the dashboard of your car this week:

   Therefore, I urge you, brothers, in view of God's mercy, to offer your bodies as living sacrifices, holy and pleasing to God—this is your spiritual act of worship. Do not conform any longer to the pattern of this world, but be transformed by the renewing of your mind. Then you will be able to test and approve what God's will is—his good, pleasing and perfect will.

   Romans 12:1–2

2. This coming week send a card, write a note of encouragement, or phone someone you know who is going through a difficult time, and encourage them in the faith.

SESSION 5
Stress From Conflict

PURPOSE To gain insight into dealing with conflict, so we can be healthier people.

AGENDA  **Gathering**   **Bible Study**   **Caring Time**

OPEN

 ## GATHERING / 15 Minutes / All Together

Leader: Read the Instructions for Step One and go first. Then read the Introduction (Step One) and explain the two Bible Study choices.

Step One: How's the Weather? Consider all the different areas of your life. Choose three areas and assign a month of the year to each one. Tell the group what season it is in each area of your life. Feel free to explain why you chose what you did.

❐ romance	❐ career	❐ relational
❐ financial	❐ spiritual	❐ family life
❐ emotional	❐ intellectual	❐ overall

JANUARY: Cold and snowy, but a new year is on the way.

FEBRUARY: Bleakest time of the year; I'm getting tired of the color gray.

MARCH: Cold and blustery, but there is a sniff of spring in the air.

APRIL: Tumultuous and stormy, but life is breaking out everywhere.

MAY: Spring has sprung! The flowers are blooming, and the skies are full of sunlight and cool breezes.

JUNE: It's pleasantly warm, things are growing, and people are beginning to take vacations.

JULY: Boy, it's hot—everything is smoldering and oppressive.

AUGUST: The heat has settled in; we sure could use some rain.

SEPTEMBER: The first cool breezes of fall can be felt, there is change in the air.

OCTOBER: Autumn has arrived; life is beginning to hibernate, but the colors are still beautiful.

NOVEMBER: The leaves have fallen and it's getting cold.

DECEMBER: Even though it's cold and desolate-looking outside, the holidays keep things festive.

Step Two: Stress From Conflict. Life would be so much easier without conflict. Nations war with nations, and people die and are maimed. Conflict in the workplace creates ulcers and unemployment. Interpersonal conflict can end friendships and marriages. Conflict between parents and children can create runaways and sleepless nights.

Conflict hurts. Conflict undermines our whole world. Conflict dulls our life. Conflict brings physical disorders, psychological stress, emotional anguish and behavioral problems. In other words, conflict brings great stress. We must deal with conflict if we are to be healthy people.

In the Option 1 Study, we see Jesus dealing with conflict (he is at odds with the religious authorities). In the Option 2 Study, Paul deals with interpersonal conflict and tries to establish some damage control. Their examples and the principles they demonstrate give us valuable insights into how we can cope with our own conflicts.

LEADER:
Choose the
OPTION 1 Bible
Study (below)
or the OPTION 2
Study (page 42).

Remember, the purpose of the Bible Study is not to talk about stress, but to talk about the issues and conflicts in your life.

 ## BIBLE STUDY / 30 Minutes / Groups of 4

Leader: Help the group decide on Option 1 or Option 2 for their Bible Study. Remember to divide into groups of 4 if there are more than 7. Ask one person in each group to be the Leader. Remind the Leader to move the group along so the Bible Study can be completed in 30 minutes.

OPTION 1

Gospel Study / Conflict Resolution
Mark 11:15–19

STUDY

Read Mark 11:15–19 and discuss your responses to the following questions with your group. As the Bible Study opens, Jesus arrives at the temple in Jerusalem and discovers that the religious establishment has set up tables and is overcharging the people.

15On reaching Jerusalem, Jesus entered the temple area and began driving out those who were buying and selling there. He overturned the tables of the money changers and the benches of those selling doves, 16and would not allow anyone to carry merchandise through the temple courts. 17And as he taught them, he said, "Is it not written:

> *" 'My house will be called*
> *a house of prayer for all nations'?*

But you have made it 'a den of robbers.' "
18The chief priests and the teachers of the law heard this and began looking for a way to kill him, for they feared him, because the whole crowd was amazed at his teaching.
19When evening came, they went out of the city.

Mark 11:15–19, NIV

1. If you had been a news reporter at the time of this event, what headline would you have used to report it?
   ❏ Visiting Prophet Vandalizes Temple: No Charges Yet Filed
   ❏ Temple Corruption Denounced: Man Claims to Represent God
   ❏ Tensions Mount Between Galilean and Chief Priests: Arrest May Be Imminent
   ❏ Gentle Galilean Prophet Turns Violent: Property Damage Is Extensive

"All men have in them an instinct for conflict, at least, all healthy men."
—Hilaire Belloc

2. Are you a little surprised to see Jesus in this passage turning over tables and driving money changers out of the temple?
   ❏ Yes—I always thought Jesus was a man of peace.
   ❏ Yes—I have been taught "peace at any price."
   ❏ Yes—maybe he could have been a little more diplomatic.
   ❏ No—I'm glad to see this story in the Bible.
   ❏ No—I know exactly how he felt.

3. Why was Jesus so angry with the merchants in the temple?
   ❏ because they weren't paying rent to use the temple
   ❏ because they were mixing capitalism and the worship of God
   ❏ because they were ignorant of what they were doing
   ❏ because they were treating a holy place as unholy

4. When your parents had conflict, were they more likely to:
   ❏ yell and throw things   ❏ hit and fight
   ❏ not speak for days   ❏ talk it over
   ❏ I don't remember any conflict. ❏ other: _____
   ❏ smile and talk sweetly between gritted teeth

5. As a child in grade school, who were you most likely to have conflict with?
   - ❏ a brother or sister
   - ❏ my father or mother
   - ❏ other friends
   - ❏ the bullies at school
   - ❏ other family members
   - ❏ no one

6. On the scale below, are you more "peace at any price" or "let's have at it"?

1	2	3	4	5	6	7	8	9	10
peace at any price									let's have at it

7. In reviewing your responses to questions 4–5, how do you think conflict in your home affected you?

8. When was the last time something happened to you that got you as angry as Jesus was about the temple? How did you react?

LEADER: When you have completed the Bible Study, move on to the Caring Time (page 45).

9. If you confronted a similar situation in your church, how do you think you would respond?
   - ❏ I would discuss the matter with the pastor and/or church board.
   - ❏ I wouldn't do anything.
   - ❏ I would ask the offending parties to leave.
   - ❏ I would pray that God would resolve the situation.

COMMENT

Things were not what they should be in the temple. This was meant to be the place where God was honored and worshiped. And yet the outer court (which was the only place pious Gentiles could worship) had been turned into a raucous oriental bazaar. Doves (which were the only sacrifice the poor could afford) cost 20 times more than the ones purchased from outside vendors. The money changers who exchanged the various coins of the Roman Empire into shekels—the only currency acceptable to pay the temple tax—charged the equivalent of one-half day's wage for this simple act. What conflict this must have caused the people! They were being taken advantage of, and yet they had no choice if they were to fulfill their religious obligations. Jesus openly and directly confronts these injustices.

Epistle Study / Interpersonal Conflict
Ephesians 4:25–32

Read Ephesians 4:25–32 and discuss your responses to the following questions with your group. This passage is part of some instructions the apostle Paul gave on what unity in the church should mean.

> [25]*Therefore each of you must put off falsehood and speak truthfully to his neighbor, for we are all members of one body.* [26]*"In your anger do not sin":* *Do not let the sun go down while you are still angry,* [27]*and do not give the devil a foothold.* [28]*He who has been stealing must steal no longer, but must work, doing something useful with his own hands, that he may have something to share with those in need.*
>
> [29]*Do not let any unwholesome talk come out of your mouths, but only what is helpful for building others up according to their needs, that it may benefit those who listen.* [30]*And do not grieve the Holy Spirit of God, with whom you were sealed for the day of redemption.* [31]*Get rid of all bitterness, rage and anger, brawling and slander, along with every form of malice.* [32]*Be kind and compassionate to one another, forgiving each other, just as in Christ God forgave you.*
>
> *Ephesians 4:25–32, NIV*

1. How would you describe Paul's tone in this Scripture passage?
   - ❐ State Department diplomat
   - ❐ Amway convention motivator
   - ❐ Marine buck sergeant in boot camp
   - ❐ Mother Teresa to new missionary recruits
   - ❐ my mother
   - ❐ other: _____

2. How would you rate yourself from 1 to 10 (1 being I NEED HELP and 10 being I'M PRETTY GOOD) in each area of this passage? Circle a number for each item. Then share your scores. There is a maximum score of 140.

   DO NOT LIE: I speak truthfully to everyone, and do not manipulate the truth for personal gain.

   I Need Help   1   2   3   4   5   6   7   8   9   10   I'm Pretty Good

   IN YOUR ANGER DO NOT SIN: My anger is appropriate at times of injustice. When I am angry, I deal with it in constructive and healthy ways.

   I Need Help   1   2   3   4   5   6   7   8   9   10   I'm Pretty Good

DO NOT LET THE SUN GO DOWN ON YOUR ANGER: When I am angry, I do everything I can to resolve my anger quickly.

I Need Help 1 2 3 4 5 6 7 8 9 10 **I'm Pretty Good**

DO NOT GIVE THE DEVIL A FOOTHOLD: I don't let my anger turn to resentment, causing a breakdown in relationship.

I Need Help 1 2 3 4 5 6 7 8 9 10 **I'm Pretty Good**

DO NOT STEAL: I don't take things which aren't mine.

I Need Help 1 2 3 4 5 6 7 8 9 10 **I'm Pretty Good**

WORK WITH YOUR HANDS, SHARE WITH THOSE IN NEED: I don't expect others to take care of me when I can take care of myself. All that I have I am willing to share with others who are in need.

I Need Help 1 2 3 4 5 6 7 8 9 10 **I'm Pretty Good**

"Happiness is not the absence of conflict, but the ability to cope with it."
—Anonymous

DO NOT LET ANY UNWHOLESOME TALK COME OUT OF YOUR MOUTH: I don't say things which are degrading. I say things which build up others.

I Need Help 1 2 3 4 5 6 7 8 9 10 **I'm Pretty Good**

DO NOT GRIEVE THE HOLY SPIRIT: I invite the Holy Spirit to move and work in my life. I want the Holy Spirit to guide and direct my life in all ways.

I Need Help 1 2 3 4 5 6 7 8 9 10 **I'm Pretty Good**

GET RID OF ALL BITTERNESS: I don't hold grudges against people.

I Need Help 1 2 3 4 5 6 7 8 9 10 **I'm Pretty Good**

GET RID OF ALL RAGE AND ANGER: I don't overreact. I get angry but seek to address the root of my anger and resolve the conflict.

I Need Help 1 2 3 4 5 6 7 8 9 10 **I'm Pretty Good**

GET RID OF BRAWLING AND SLANDER: I don't assert myself loudly in arguments. I don't speak ill of anyone, whether or not I like them as a person.

I Need Help 1 2 3 4 5 6 7 8 9 10 **I'm Pretty Good**

GET RID OF EVERY FORM OF MALICE: I don't have a desire to plot against others, or to see them suffer.

I Need Help 1 2 3 4 5 6 7 8 9 10 **I'm Pretty Good**

BE KIND AND COMPASSIONATE: I am generous in all the ways I can be. And I show mercy to those who do not deserve it.

I Need Help 1 2 3 4 5 6 7 8 9 10 **I'm Pretty Good**

FORGIVE EACH OTHER: I will forgive someone when they have wronged me, even if they don't ask me for my forgiveness.

I Need Help 1 2 3 4 5 6 7 8 9 10 **I'm Pretty Good**

LEADER: When you have completed the Bible Study, move on to the Caring Time (on page 45).

3. How do you handle interpersonal conflict? Give a recent example.
   - ❐ I let the pressure build up.
   - ❐ I ignore all conflict until I explode.
   - ❐ I pray for God's intervention.
   - ❐ I immediately confront and resolve the problem.
   - ❐ I involve a third person in conflict resolution.
   - ❐ I absorb the stress from conflict.
   - ❐ other: _____

4. When in your life (and with whom) have you had your greatest interpersonal conflict?
   - ❐ during childhood
   - ❐ during adolescence
   - ❐ during young adulthood
   - ❐ during middle adulthood
   - ❐ during late adulthood
   - ❐ with in-laws
   - ❐ with God
   - ❐ with boss
   - ❐ with coworker
   - ❐ with children
   - ❐ with self
   - ❐ with spouse
   - ❐ with parents
   - ❐ with brother/sister
   - ❐ with friend(s)
   - ❐ with teacher/coach
   - ❐ with government
   - ❐ other: _____

CARING TIME / 15–45 Minutes / All Together

Leader: Bring all of the foursomes back together for a time of caring support for each other through Sharing, Prayer and Action. Be sensitive to what others may share during this time.

SHARING

In light of our Bible Study on stress from conflicts, briefly share with the group either a conflict you are presently in or a conflict of which you are aware. For example: "Please pray for me and my son," or "Please pray for my spouse and her/his boss."

PRAYER

Remembering the requests which were just shared, close with a prayer time. The Leader can start a conversational prayer (short phrases and sentences) with group members following. After an appropriate amount of time, the Leader can close the time of prayer by praying for any requests not already mentioned.

ACTION

1. Write down this Scripture on a 3" x 5" card to memorize this week:

   Do not let any unwholesome talk come out of your mouths, but only what is helpful for building others up according to their needs, that it may benefit those who listen.
   Ephesians 4:29

2. These are the necessary steps in dealing with conflict in our lives: confront the issue, identify the problem, get perspective on it, and claim what is yours in Christ. Applying these steps to a conflict you are presently in, prayerfully outline a course of action you will take this week to resolve the conflict.

   Use these questions to help you in planning your course of action:

   • Who are the participants in the conflict and how did the conflict begin?
   • What is the root problem?
   • What would an outside observer say is going on?
   • What resources do you have to deal with the problem?
   • What is one concrete step you could have taken (or need to take now)?

   For example: "I will go to my boss and discuss with him/her my difficulty with their new procedures." Or "I will call my friend whom I haven't talked with since our 'blowup' three months ago and see if we can resolve our differences."

   As you feel comfortable, ask one or more group members to remember you in prayer throughout the week as you attempt to bring resolution to a conflict in your life.

SESSION 6
Stress From Loss

PURPOSE To see that although loss can be painful, it can bring about a greater understanding of life.

AGENDA  Gathering   Bible Study   Caring Time

OPEN

GATHERING / 15 Minutes / All Together

Leader: There is probably nothing more difficult for people than to sustain a loss. So continue to be sensitive to all who share. By this time, group members should feel comfortable enough with each other to share at a deeper level. Read the instructions for Step One and go first. Then read the Introduction (Step Two) and explain the choices for Bible Study.

Step One: Ups and Downs. Our lives have their good times and their bad times. Help your group get to know you better by charting your life. From your birth to the present, mark the good times and bad times in your life. Feel free to explain some of these ups and downs to your group.

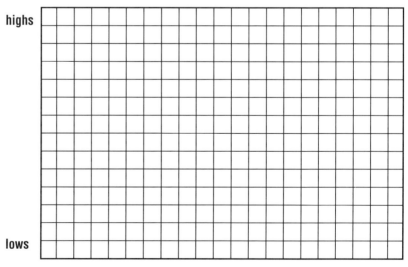

highs

lows

birth   present

Step Two: Stress Loss. It is nearly impossible to go through life without experiencing at least one major loss. Some people lose their health; others lose money and security; still others lose their freedom or self-respect. But perhaps the most painful loss of all is to lose a loved one— a child, a friend, a spouse or a parent. Loss can produce some of the most intense stress we may ever experience. In this session, we will deal with loss as a major contributor to stress.

In Option 1, we will see how the loss of hope affected two of Jesus' disciples. We will look at two people (in Luke's Gospel) who lost their faith after the Crucifixion. And for those taking the Option 2 Study, we will see the apostle Paul's reaction when he was not in control of his world. While a time of loss can be a stressful and painful experience, it can also bring a greater understanding of life.

LEADER:
Choose the
OPTION 1 Bible
Study (below)
or the OPTION 2
Study (page 51).

Remember in this session the issue is your life. Use the Scripture passages to walk into your story with your group.

 # BIBLE STUDY / 30 Minutes / Groups of 4

Leader: Help the group choose an Option for study. Divide into groups of 4 for discussion. Remind the Leader for each foursome to move the group along so the Bible Study can be completed in the time allotted. Have everyone return together for the Caring Time for the final 15–45 minutes.

OPTION 1

Gospel Study / Lost and Found
Luke 24:13–35

STUDY

Read Luke 24:13–35 and discuss your responses to the following questions with your group. Remember that this passage begins immediately following the Resurrection. But the disciples in this story do not know it has happened.

¹³Now that same day two of them [Jesus' disciples] were going to a village called Emmaus, about seven miles from Jerusalem. ¹⁴They were talking with each other about everything that had happened. ¹⁵As they talked and discussed these things with each other, Jesus himself came up and walked along with them; ¹⁶but they were kept from recognizing him.
¹⁷He asked them, "What are you discussing together as you walk along?" They stood still, their faces downcast. ¹⁸One of them, named Cleopas, asked him, "Are you only a visitor to Jerusalem and do not know the things that have happened there in these days?"
¹⁹"What things?" he asked.

"About Jesus of Nazareth," they replied. "He was a prophet, powerful in word and deed before God and all the people. ²⁰The chief priests and our rulers handed him over to be sentenced to death, and they crucified him; ²¹but we had hoped that he was the one who was going to redeem Israel. And what is more, it is the third day since all this took place. ²²In addition, some of our women amazed us. They went to the tomb early this morning ²³but didn't find his body. They came and told us that they had seen a vision of angels, who said he was alive. ²⁴Then some of our companions went to the tomb and found it just as the women had said, but him they did not see."

²⁵He said to them, "How foolish you are, and how slow of heart to believe all that the prophets have spoken! ²⁶Did not the Christ have to suffer these things and then enter his glory?" ²⁷And beginning with Moses and all the Prophets, he explained to them what was said in all the Scriptures concerning himself.

²⁸As they approached the village to which they were going, Jesus acted as if he were going farther. ²⁹But they urged him strongly, "Stay with us, for it is nearly evening; the day is almost over." So he went in to stay with them.

³⁰When he was at the table with them, he took bread, gave thanks, broke it and began to give it to them. ³¹Then their eyes were opened and they recognized him, and he disappeared from their sight. ³²They asked each other, "Were not our hearts burning within us while he talked with us on the road and opened the Scriptures to us?"

³³They got up and returned at once to Jerusalem. There they found the Eleven and those with them, assembled together ³⁴and saying, "It is true! The Lord has risen and has appeared to Simon." ³⁵Then the two told what had happened on the way, and how Jesus was recognized by them when he broke the bread.

Luke 24:13–35, NIV

1. What surprises you most about the two disciples at the beginning of this story?
   - ❒ They would leave town before finding out what happened to Jesus.
   - ❒ They were in the room when "our women" reported on the empty tomb, and didn't put two and two together.
   - ❒ I am not surprised at all, because I do the same thing in many ways today.

2. If you could put in a good word for these two disciples, what would it be?
   - ❒ They had been through a lot in the last three days.
   - ❒ They didn't know the Scriptures well.
   - ❒ They were a little impulsive.
   - ❒ They needed to get away for a few days.
   - ❒ other: _____

3. Do you think Jesus could have been a little more understanding with these two confused disciples?
   ❑ Well, he was a little harsh with them.
   ❑ No, I think they deserved it.
   ❑ He wasn't harsh—he was their counselor.
   ❑ other: _____

"Faith draws the poison from every grief, takes the sting from every loss, and quenches the fire of every pain; and only faith can do it."
—Josiah Gilbert Holland

4. When do you think the healing started to take place in their lives?
   ❑ when they started to verbalize their disillusionment
   ❑ when Jesus explained the Scripture to them
   ❑ when their hearts started to "burn"
   ❑ when they went back to the fellowship in the Upper Room and shared their story

5. When was the last time you felt like throwing in the towel and leaving any commitments to job, family or faith?
   ❑ when I was jilted
   ❑ years ago
   ❑ the other day
   ❑ I never have.

6. What has God used to restore your faith and renew your spirit in a time of great loss?
   ❑ a fellowship of caring people
   ❑ time away to be with God
   ❑ talking out my pain with a trusted friend/counselor
   ❑ I have never experienced loss to this degree.

LEADER: When you have completed the Bible Study, move on to the Caring Time (page 54).

7. If Jesus were to suddenly come alongside you today and walk for seven miles with you, what do you think he would talk about … or let you talk about?
   ❑ some of the struggles I am going through right now
   ❑ my family situation
   ❑ my job
   ❑ He probably wouldn't say a word. He would just be there.
   ❑ I don't know. I really don't know.

COMMENT

Like these disciples, we also understand the experience of pinning our hopes on what we know is certain to take place in the future: a great job will materialize, a wonderful spouse will appear, our children will succeed. But it doesn't always happen that way. Someone else is offered the job; the person you love doesn't feel the same way about you; your child drops out of school and lives off others. What once seemed so bright is now dull and tarnished. The dreams die. Energy fades. Where once there was hope, now there is despair. Is there any way to recover hope?

In this story, the hope that was lost is that Jesus would redeem Israel; that he would fulfill all of God's promises to them; and that they would once again become a great people. All of this was shattered by a Roman cross. But something happens to the two travelers. They who were "downcast" now feel their "hearts burning" within them. Hope rises again.

Jesus will open your eyes to new hope.

What happened? What brought about the change? In this passage, first they articulated what their hopes had been. Second, they found that the answer to their dashed hopes was there with them all along. They just did not see it yet. Third, their eyes were opened by Jesus. He gave them new hope.

There is insight for us here. It would be wrong to suggest that all loss is merely a matter of not knowing the facts (in this case, that Jesus had been resurrected), and that things will be all right when they are made known. It is true, however, that the shock of loss often paralyzes our vision so that we see only what we have lost, and not what we have. We need new eyes to see our loss in its full context. How does this new vision come? It comes from Jesus. He brings us words of wisdom and insight (through Scripture and his people). It is he who also gives us the gift of life. His resurrection life is our resurrection life. As we touch that Life, we recover our life.

Epistle Study / Ultimate Hope
Romans 8:18–25,31–39

Read Romans 8:18–25,31–39 and share your responses to the following questions with your group. This is a passage of encouragement which Paul wrote to Christians in Rome.

> *18I consider that our present sufferings are not worth comparing with the glory that will be revealed in us. 19The creation waits in eager expectation for the sons of God to be revealed. 20For the creation was subjected to frustration, not by its own choice, but by the will of the one who subjected it, in hope 21that the creation itself will be liberated from its bondage to decay and brought into the glorious freedom of the children of God.*
>
> *22We know that the whole creation has been groaning as in the pains of childbirth right up to the present time. 23Not only so, but we ourselves, who have the firstfruits of the Spirit, groan inwardly as we wait eagerly for our adoption as sons, the redemption of our bodies. 24For in this hope we were saved. But hope that is seen is no hope at all. Who hopes for what he already has? 25But if we hope for what we do not yet have, we wait for it patiently. ...*
>
> *31What, then, shall we say in response to this? If God is for us, who can be against us? 32He who did not spare his own Son, but gave him up for us all—how will he not also, along with him, graciously give us all things? 33Who will bring any charge against those whom God has chosen? It is God who justifies. 34Who is he that condemns? Christ Jesus, who died—more than that, who was raised to life—is at the right hand of God and is also interceding for us. 35Who shall separate us from the love of Christ? Shall trouble or hardship or persecution or famine or nakedness or danger or sword? 36As it is written:*
>
> > *"For your sake we face death all day long;*
> > *we are considered as sheep to be slaughtered."*
>
> *37No, in all these things we are more than conquerors through him who loved us. 38For I am convinced that neither death nor life, neither angels nor demons, neither the present nor the future, nor any powers, 39neither height nor depth, nor anything else in all creation, will be able to separate us from the love of God that is in Christ Jesus our Lord.*
>
> *Romans 8:18–25,31–39, NIV*

1. If you had been one of the small band of Christians in Rome and faced the possibility of losing your life, your job, your family and friends because of your commitment to Christ, what would be your response to these words from Paul?
   ❏ Easy for him to say.
   ❏ Right on—that is just what I needed!
   ❏ I believe all of this, but it doesn't take away how I feel.
   ❏ God, can you make it a little bit easier?

2. When Paul compares the suffering of this world to the pain of child-birth (v. 22), what does that do to your attitude toward suffering?
   ❏ It depresses me—childbirth is the most painful thing that I can think of.
   ❏ It uplifts me—childbirth pain results in new life.
   ❏ It makes me skeptical—I don't see the new life coming.
   ❏ other: _____

"God will not look you over for medals, degrees, or diplomas, but for scars."
—Elbert Hubbard

3. At what age did you first experience the loss of someone or something important to you? What was that loss?
   ❏ loss/death of a pet   ❏ death of a relative/friend
   ❏ loss of a favorite teacher   ❏ loss of a close friend
   ❏ moving from old neighborhood   ❏ loss of a favorite toy
   ❏ loss of a girl/boyfriend   ❏ divorce of parents

4. What is the most significant loss you have experienced in your life?
   ❏ loss of loved one   ❏ loss of job
   ❏ loss of freedom   ❏ loss of hope
   ❏ loss of money   ❏ loss of friend(s)
   ❏ loss of security   ❏ loss of self-respect
   ❏ loss of home   ❏ loss of marriage
   ❏ loss of health   ❏ other: _____

5. What were your feelings about this loss? (Check two or three.)
   ❏ helplessness   ❏ anxiety   ❏ grief
   ❏ despair   ❏ sadness   ❏ worry
   ❏ loneliness   ❏ shock   ❏ depression
   ❏ bewilderment   ❏ fear   ❏ sorrow
   ❏ anger   ❏ guilt   ❏ confusion
   ❏ heartbreak   ❏ anguish   ❏ hopelessness

6. What is the closest you have come to feeling abandoned? How can this passage of Scripture help you in such a time?

LEADER: When you have completed the Bible Study, move on to the Caring Time (page 54).

7. In light of Paul's promise (that we can be more than conquerors over the powers that threaten us with loss), how well are you living out that promise?
   ❐ poorly—I've raised the white flag.
   ❐ not so good—I'm hanging in there, but I'm surrounded.
   ❐ okay—The promise of victory is keeping me going.
   ❐ great—Victory is sure.

8. What needs to be the next step you take to "rally the troops"?

COMMENT

Suffering and glory are two concepts Paul wrestles with in Romans 8:18–27. Pain and promise; agony and ecstasy; problems and hope. We all are aware of the stark contrast. Athletes train tirelessly—often at great personal expense—all in hope of winning the big event. Or take Paul's image of childbearing. Although there are few forms of such intense pain, millions of women eagerly bear children each year. It is the hope of children which makes the pain bearable.

But do we know about this suffering/glory combination Paul presents in terms of spiritual reality? Are we as motivated by the hope of redemption as we are by the hope of winning a game or bearing a child?

Then Paul leaves behind all the gloom, despair and suffering, and captivates his audience with his glorious vision of Christians who are "more than conquerors" (8:28–39). These words give us hope, no matter what our circumstances (or losses) in life might be.

CARING TIME / 15–45 Minutes / All Together

Leader: Bring all of the foursomes back together for a time of caring support for each other through Sharing, Prayer and Action. Be sensitive to what others share.

SHARING

Take a look at the list below and choose one thing that you are going to do for yourself before your next meeting. Take turns telling your group what you have chosen. At your next meeting, your group is going to ask you if you took care of yourself the way you planned.

Before our next meeting, I am going to take care of myself by ...

❑ getting a massage
❑ buying a new outfit of clothes
❑ splurging on a gourmet dinner
❑ having a slumber party
❑ buying fresh-cut flowers
❑ buying the gadget I've wanted
❑ sitting poolside and enjoying the sun
❑ organizing the closet, desk, garage or bookshelves
❑ grabbing a friend and doing something I've always wanted to do
❑ cutting out the TV, junk food, tobacco or alcohol

❑ taking a trip
❑ taking a personal retreat
❑ making my favorite dessert
❑ getting a facial/manicure
❑ praying for __ minutes daily
❑ walking/running ___ miles

PRAYER

Go around the circle, praying for the person on your left. Pray that they will find God's loving-kindness even as they feel their loss. If someone is uncomfortable praying aloud, they can pray silently. Say "Amen" when you are finished so the next person will know to continue.

ACTION

1. Write on a 3" x 5" card the Scripture verses below and memorize them this week:

   For I am convinced that neither death nor life, neither angels nor demons, neither the present nor the future, nor any powers, neither height nor depth, nor anything else in all creation, will be able to separate us from the love of God that is in Christ Jesus our Lord.
   Romans 8:38–39

2. Plan two or three concrete steps you can take this week to help resolve one of the areas of concern you mentioned in the Sharing Time above.

SESSION 7
Stress From Overload

PURPOSE | To identify the signs of overload and learn corrective steps.

AGENDA |  **Gathering**   **Bible Study**   **Caring Time**

OPEN | ## GATHERING / 15 Minutes / All Together

Leader: This is the final session together. You may want to have your Caring Time first. If not, be sure to allow a full 25 minutes at the end of the session. Read the instructions for Step One and set the pace by going first. Then read the Introduction (Step Two) and move on to the Bible Study.

Step One: What I Need Right Now ... Choose five things from this list that you think you need more of. Tell the group why you chose what you did. This is adapted from *Structured Exercises in Wellness Promotion*, Tubesing and Tubesing, eds., Whole Person Press, 1983.

❐ vitality	❐ self-esteem	❐ direction
❐ tenderness	❐ composure	❐ security
❐ recognition	❐ generosity	❐ balance
❐ activity	❐ confidence	❐ caring
❐ awareness	❐ health	❐ motivation
❐ sharing	❐ solitude	❐ devotion
❐ contemplation	❐ serenity	❐ trust
❐ insight	❐ joy	❐ commitment
❐ communion	❐ integration	❐ forgiveness
❐ surrender	❐ faith	❐ purpose
❐ music	❐ laughter	❐ support
❐ self-expression	❐ companionship	❐ harmony
❐ romance	❐ intimacy	❐ patience
❐ beauty	❐ sensitivity	❐ self-awareness
❐ skill	❐ opportunity	❐ challenges
❐ variety	❐ structure	❐ accomplishments
❐ control	❐ imagination	❐ money
❐ responsibility	❐ education	❐ experience
❐ freedom	❐ strength	❐ energy
❐ fitness	❐ relaxation	❐ comfort
❐ nutrition	❐ touching	❐ sleep

Step Two: Stress From Overload. Over the past several decades, the word "burnout" has come into common usage. Burnout is the state of physical, intellectual, emotional, and spiritual exhaustion. In contemporary society, burnout has reached epidemic proportions. It is most evident in people in the helping professions—nurses, social workers, teachers, doctors and ministers. None of us is immune from the debilitating effects of burnout. Athletes and coaches burn out from the wear-and-tear of intense competition. Parents burn out from the pressures of providing for their families.

LEADER:
Choose the
OPTION 1 Bible
Study (below)
or the OPTION 2
Study (page 60).

In the Option 1 Study, we see Jesus on the verge of overload as he contemplates his impending suffering and death. We can learn much from the way he handles his distress. And in the Option 2 Study (from 2 Corinthians), Paul shows how the "God of all comfort" can help us to avoid overload.

 # BIBLE STUDY / 25 Minutes / Groups of 4

Leader: For this final session, divide into groups of 4 (if there are more than 7 in your group). Help the groups choose their Bible Study. Remind the Leaders to end their Bible Study time five minutes earlier than usual to allow ample time for your final Caring Time—deciding what the group will do next.

OPTION 1

Gospel Study / Wear and Tear
Matthew 26:36–46

STUDY

Read Matthew 26:36–46 and discuss your responses to the following questions with your group. This passage reflects Jesus' anguish over his imminent crucifixion. The heart of his prayer was for God's will to be accomplished, whatever the cost.

³⁶Then Jesus went with his disciples to a place called Gethsemane, and he said to them, "Sit here while I go over there and pray." ³⁷He took Peter and the two sons of Zebedee along with him, and he began to be sorrowful and troubled. ³⁸Then he said to them, "My soul is overwhelmed with sorrow to the point of death. Stay here and keep watch with me."

³⁹Going a little farther, he fell with his face to the ground and prayed, "My Father, if it is possible, may this cup be taken from me. Yet not as I will, but as you will."

⁴⁰Then he returned to his disciples and found them sleeping. "Could you men not keep watch with me for one hour?" he asked Peter. ⁴¹"Watch and pray so that you will not fall into temptation. The spirit is willing, but the body is weak."

42He went away a second time and prayed, "My Father, if it is not possible for this cup to be taken away unless I drink it, may your will be done."

43When he came back, he again found them sleeping, because their eyes were heavy. 44So he left them and went away once more and prayed the third time, saying the same thing.

45Then he returned to the disciples and said to them, "Are you still sleeping and resting? Look, the hour is near, and the Son of Man is betrayed into the hands of sinners. 46Rise, let us go! Here comes my betrayer!"

Matthew 26:36–46, NIV

1. What strikes you as the most surprising aspect of this story?
   - ❒ that the disciples would sleep when Jesus obviously needed them
   - ❒ that even Jesus could get this stressed out
   - ❒ that Jesus gave them a second and third chance, and they still failed
   - ❒ Nothing—it all seems very human.

2. Why do you think Jesus chose Peter and James and John ("the two sons of Zebedee")—as opposed to the other disciples— to be with him in this hour of sorrow?
   - ❒ He trusted them more.
   - ❒ He knew they were going to be future church leaders.
   - ❒ They were his best friends.
   - ❒ They just happened to be near when he was looking around for someone.

"How to cope with stress: Rule #1 is, don't sweat the small stuff. Rule #2 is, it's all small stuff."
—Dr. Robert Eliot

3. What would you have done if you had been with Jesus at Gethsemane?
   - ❒ I probably would have slept too.
   - ❒ I would have been attentive to his every command.
   - ❒ I probably would have gone home to bed.
   - ❒ I would have done what he asked, even though I didn't understand it.

4. Which of these common symptoms of overload did Jesus exhibit?
   - ❒ irritability   ❒ disappointment
   - ❒ anxiety   ❒ annoyance
   - ❒ depression   ❒ exhaustion
   - ❒ fatigue   ❒ agitation
   - ❒ sleeplessness

5. When you were in high school, who did you turn to when you needed support in a tough situation? What qualities did this person have which made you turn to him or her?

6. When you face a time of stress overload now (as Jesus faced in Gethsemane), what do you look for most from your friends?

7. What importance does prayer have in this passage?
   ❐ Prayer gave Jesus a chance to state his hesitancy to his Father
   ❐ Prayer gave Jesus the support he needed in his agony.
   ❐ Prayer gave him a reason to get away from the disciples.
   ❐ Prayer would solve all of Jesus' problems.

8. What changes in Jesus' attitude take place in this passage?
   ❐ He moves from fear and anxiety to acceptance of his fate.
   ❐ He moves from a defensive posture to an offensive posture.
   ❐ He moves from anger and annoyance with the disciples to resignation and acceptance of their behavior.
   ❐ He moves from "wanting out" to accepting and fulfilling his mission as Savior.

9. What changes in your attitude need to take place?

LEADER: When you have completed the Bible Study, move on to the Caring Time (page 63).

10. These were the ways Jesus coped with and overcame burnout. Which ways would you find helpful?
    ❐ praying to his heavenly Father for strength and support
    ❐ appealing to the disciples (friends) for support
    ❐ accepting the reality of the situation
    ❐ acknowledging his feelings and moving ahead

COMMENT

The stages of burnout.

Burnout comes on as a fizzle and not an explosion. It is important that we identify and understand burnout. There are four stages in the burnout process. Stage 1 usually starts with a new beginning, such as our first "real" job or getting married. It is a time of high idealism, high enthusiasm and high energy. After a period of time, our high idealism and energy starts to grate against unexpected realism. We enter Stage 2, where we experience a decrease in energy and enthusiasm. We become more physically and emotionally tired. We also become more detached from people we care about. If there is no intervention, no slowing or stopping this slide down the slippery slope of burnout, we move to a more serious state—Stage 3. This stage is characterized by chronic exhaustion.

Now we are physically and emotionally exhausted at the end of the day. And sleep, if it comes, is interrupted and without its restorative purpose. During Stage 3, we may also experience diffuse physical symptoms, such as headaches, heart palpitations, increased blood pressure or chronic stomach upset. Emotionally, we are irritable with almost everyone. Again, if there is no intervention, we move to Stage 4, the most serious stage. This stage is a time of crisis where we are obsessed with our own problems. We can think of nothing else except what is happening to us. We become apathetic and try to avoid work. We become impersonal, detached and unsympathetic toward other people. Physically, our nagging symptoms may become more serious and even life-threatening. In short, we are physically, emotionally and spiritually worn out.

On the following diagram of the Slippery Slope of Burnout, place an "✘" at the stage that best represents where you are in the burnout process. Share your response with your group.

Slippery Slope of Burnout

Stage 1—
• high energy
• high enthusiasm
• high idealism

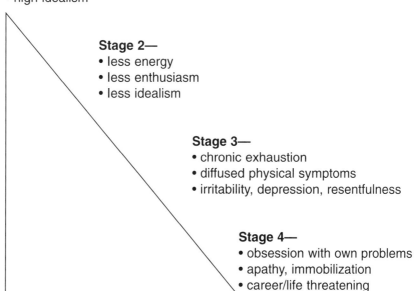

Stage 2—
• less energy
• less enthusiasm
• less idealism

Stage 3—
• chronic exhaustion
• diffused physical symptoms
• irritability, depression, resentfulness

Stage 4—
• obsession with own problems
• apathy, immobilization
• career/life threatening

Epistle Study / Beating Overload
2 Corinthians 1:3–11

STUDY

Read 2 Corinthians 1:3–11 and discuss your responses to the following questions with your group. The apostle Paul had to undergo great hardships to establish some churches. One of those churches was in Corinth. In this passage, he tells them about some of his experiences.

³Praise be to the God and Father of our Lord Jesus Christ, the Father of compassion and the God of all comfort, ⁴who comforts us in all our troubles, so that we can comfort those in any trouble with the comfort we ourselves have received from God. ⁵For just as the sufferings of Christ flow over into our lives, so also through Christ our comfort overflows. ⁶If we are distressed, it is for your comfort and salvation; if we are comforted, it is for your comfort, which produces in you patient endurance of the same sufferings we suffer. ⁷And our hope for you is firm, because we know that just as you share in our sufferings, so also you share in our comfort.

⁸We do not want you to be uninformed, brothers, about the hardships we suffered in the province of Asia. We were under great pressure, far beyond our ability to endure, so that we despaired even of life. ⁹Indeed, in our heart we felt the sentence of death. But this happened that we might not rely on ourselves but on God, who raises the dead. ¹⁰He has delivered us from such a deadly peril, and he will deliver us. On him we have set our hope that he will continue to deliver us, ¹¹as you help us by your prayers. Then many will give thanks on our behalf for the gracious favor granted us in answer to the prayers of many.

2 Corinthians 1:3–11, NIV

1. If you had been one of the recipients of this letter, what would you have asked Paul the first time you saw him after hearing these words?
   ❐ What were the hardships in Asia all about?
   ❐ Why is your hope for us so firm?
   ❐ Why do you go through all of this for us?
   ❐ How can you always praise God when things get hard?

2. When you were upset as a child, who comforted you?
   ❐ my mother/father   ❐ my best friend
   ❐ my grandparents   ❐ I didn't turn to anyone for comfort.
   ❐ my sister/brother   ❐ other: _____

*"To be willing to
suffer in order to
create is one
thing; to realize
that one's
creation
necessitates
one's suffering,
that suffering is
one of the
greatest of
God's gifts, is
almost to reach
a mystical solu-
tion of the
problem of evil."*
—J. W. M.
Sullivan

3. Because God comforts us, we can comfort other people. How would you try to comfort someone who was distressed?
   - ❏ I would listen to them.
   - ❏ I would pray for/with them.
   - ❏ I would tell them God will take care of them.
   - ❏ I would tell them that they need more faith.
   - ❏ I would tell them that they need to take control of their life.
   - ❏ I wouldn't feel comfortable doing this.

4. What effect can stress or distress have in a Christian's life?
   - ❏ Christians don't have stress in their lives.
   - ❏ Stress makes a Christian dependent on God.
   - ❏ Stress makes a Christian overly dependent on others.
   - ❏ Stress causes one to question their faith.
   - ❏ other: _____

5. When have you felt like Paul did in verses 8 and 9?

6. When a Christian experiences distress and overload, what can he or she do?
   - ❏ confess the sin and start over
   - ❏ give up on God
   - ❏ talk to others
   - ❏ Real Christians don't get "overloaded."
   - ❏ pray and seek God's wisdom and comfort

7. When has your suffering resulted in something positive for others (see v. 6) or for yourself (see v. 9)?

8. Often we do not recognize overload until we are too worn down to do much about it. The following exercise will help you determine if you are currently experiencing overload. (If you are comfortable, share the results with your group.)

   Instructions: Indicate how frequently you experience each of the following statements. Use the scale below to rate each statement.

0 = almost never	2 = frequently
1 = infrequently	3 = almost always

   _____ I am irritable with others (family, coworkers, etc.).

   _____ I feel emotionally drained by my work.

   _____ I have difficulty falling asleep at night.

_____ I lack motivation in my work.

_____ I am disillusioned with my work (including housework).

_____ I think, "Why don't people leave me alone?"

_____ I treat people more impersonally than I would like.

_____ I wake up tired and have difficulty facing another day.

_____ I consider myself a failure.

_____ I am bothered by stress-related ailments (such as indigestion, headaches, high blood pressure, etc.).

LEADER: When you have completed the Bible Study, move on to the Caring Time (page 63).

_____ I feel like I am at the end of my rope.

_____ I feel trapped in my work.

_____ I feel exhausted at the end of the workday.

_____ I feel people make a lot of demands on me.

_____ I feel unfulfilled and am dissatisfied with my life.

_____ Total

Total your score. A score of 0–15 indicates that you are probably not experiencing overload. A score of 16–30 indicates that you are probably experiencing moderate overload (and should do something about it). A score of 31–45 indicates that you are probably experiencing severe overload (and definitely should do something about it).

COMMENT

Our tendency is to look at suffering as a sign of divine displeasure. In the early church, however, it was seen as the mark of the Christian. In the same way that our Lord suffered, so we too, as his people, may be called to suffer.

We are not to court suffering, nor is suffering good in itself. Suffering is not abnormal in this world, and God can use such suffering on our behalf. The implication is that suffering brings stress; but suffering (and stress) can be transcended, in part, by opening ourselves to the redemptive meaning of it.

CARING TIME / 15–45 Minutes / All Together

Leader: This is decision time. This questionnaire is designed to help you evaluate your group experience and to decide about the future. Then you may want to plan a special time of prayer to conclude this course.

EVALUATION

Take a few minutes to review your experience and reflect. Go around on each point and finish the sentences.

1. I have learned the following about stress in my life from this series of Bible studies:

2. As I see it, our purpose and goal as a group was to:

3. We achieved our goal(s):
   ❑ completely   ❑ somewhat
   ❑ almost completely   ❑ We blew it.

4. The high point in this course for me has been:
   ❑ the Scripture exercises
   ❑ the sharing
   ❑ discovering myself
   ❑ belonging to a real community of love
   ❑ finding new life and purpose for my life
   ❑ the fun of the fellowship

5. One of the most significant things I learned was:

6. In my opinion, our group functioned:
   ❑ smoothly, and we grew
   ❑ pretty well, but we didn't grow
   ❑ It was tough, but we grew.
   ❑ It was tough, and we didn't grow.

7. The thing I appreciated most about the group as a whole is:

CONTINUATION

Do you want to continue as a group? If so, what do you need to improve? Finish the sentence:

> *"If I were to suggest one thing we could work on as a group, it would be ..."*

MAKE A COVENANT

A covenant is a promise made to each other in the presence of God. Its purpose is to indicate your intention to make yourselves available to one another for the fulfillment of the purposes you share in common. In a spirit of prayer, work your way through the following sentences, trying to reach an agreement on each statement pertaining to your ongoing life together. Write out your covenant like a contract, stating your purpose, goals, and the ground rules for your group.

1. The purpose of our group will be ... (finish the sentence)

2. Our goals will be ...

3. We will meet for _____weeks, after which we will decide if we wish to continue as a group.

4. We will meet from _____ to _____ and we will strive to start on time and end on time.

5. We will meet at _____ (place) or we will rotate from house to house.

6. We will agree to the following ground rules for our group (check):

   ❐ PRIORITY: While you are in the course, you give the group meetings priority.

   ❐ PARTICIPATION: Everyone participates and no one dominates.

   ❐ RESPECT: Everyone is given the right to their own opinion, and "dumb questions" are encouraged and respected.

   ❐ CONFIDENTIALITY: Anything that is said in the meeting is never repeated outside the meeting.

   ❐ EMPTY CHAIR: The group stays open to new people at every meeting, as long as they understand the ground rules.

   ❐ SUPPORT: Permission is given to call upon each other in time of need at any time.

   ❐ ACCOUNTABILITY: We agree to let the members of the group hold us accountable to the commitments which each of us make in whatever loving ways we decide upon.

If you decide to continue as a group for a few more weeks, what are you going to use for study and discipline? There are 15 other studies available at this 201 Series level. 301 Courses are for deeper Bible Study, also with Study Notes.

For more information about small group resources and possible directions, please contact your small group coordinator or SERENDIPITY at 1-800-525-9563 or visit us at: www.serendipityhouse.com.